To D

DYLAN'S GOWER

with best wishes

Robert Edward Gurney

Blwyddyn newydd
dda 2016.

LLYFRAU
CAMBRIA

Published in the United Kingdom in 2014 by
Cambria Books, Wales, United Kingdom

Original cover design © William Gurney

Introduction

The Ballad of Three Cliffs Bay

to Paddy, who helps me without knowing it
to my friend Robert Gurney, who believes in me
to Dylan Thomas, my memories intact.

I don't know why Dylan drove me to it
I suppose that it was a joke
one of those that he knew how to play

I don't remember much, about that night
except falling into the sea
wet clothes
cigarettes floating among seaweed

the sound of the waves
the improvised fire among the rocks
and the old hip flask, slipping
from my fingers.

I would like to go back to those days
when we devoured eternity
when the dream of living
had not destroyed us

when I was happy,
still floating drowned in the sea.

Andrés Bohoslavsky
(Translated from the Spanish by Robert Edward
Gurney)

Author's Prologue

Talking to Dylan Thomas's lovely granddaughter, Hannah Ellis, and to the inspiring Olivier Award-winning actor Guy Masterson last night at the RSA in John Street, London on the occasion of their brilliant British Council seminar "Dylan Thomas: A Life in Words", I was particularly struck by Hannah's reference to Dylan's notebooks which he wrote between the ages of fifteen and twenty. She mentioned how these had been lying mouldering in a box in Boulder, America, but are now available to the public in Swansea.

Hannah argued that everything was there, in embryo, in those notebooks, that that period of poetic creativity, those five years of "cosseted" (Hannah's word) creative activity, a veritable explosion that occurred within the young genius relieved to drop out early, at sixteen, from a school in which he was bored, were the foundations of his work to come. Dylan lived in Swansea, on the edge of Gower, during those years. Hannah referred to a text in which he wrote that he "often" went down to Gower.

The gist of this book, Dylan's Gower, is that it is clearly time to re-evaluate the influence of the spectacular and quirky Gower Peninsula on his work. Hannah maintained that Newquay and Laugharne were key periods in the gestation of Under Milk Wood. I agreed but argued that to them must be added the beautiful bays and villages of his early 'backyard', the place to which he would escape during his formative years and to which he was tempted to 'retire' in the final year of his life. This book points, perhaps, to the need to re-evaluate the role Gower played in the formation of the creatures of the mysterious entity of Dylan's literary imagination.

Robert Edward Gurney, St Albans, October 2014

THE POEMS

1

2

Infinity

to Arthur Rimbaud

Sitting high up

on the cliff

at Worm's Head,

I watch

the sun setting.

A red stain

is vanishing

behind a curtain of grey.

Little by little

the sea disappears.

The sea leaves

with the sun,

whispers Rimbaud.

The Mist

to Thomas Gray (1716-1771)
and Vernon Watkins (1906-1967)

The sea-mist rolls in
obliterating the landscape.

The first to go is the sea,
then sand dunes as big as pyramids.

It creeps up the road
erasing The Captain's Table
and The Ship
where Dylan once drank.

The tree tops disappear,
then the cliffs.

All that is left
are some marks in the sky,
the crows that are hovering
without moving.

And through the mist can be heard

as clear as the church bell

the sad tolling of the buoy

in Overton Mere.

The Crows

to Vincent Van Gogh

The inhabitants of Port Eynon
have a nickname,
they are called 'the crows'.

There are some tall, scrawny fir trees
on the cliff above our house
full of crows that fly up
into the teeth of the wind.

They call out over The Ship
where Dylan drank
and watched them through the portholes
planning a night of passion.

Their caws are dark stains
on the transparent air
that whips the village.

Sitting by the fire
we can hear their cries
coming down the chimney.

They make us think of Vincent
and the temptation
to brave the elements.

The Fires

I can still see them,
the fires on the beach
in the Bay.

In the dark they look
strange, almost prehistoric,
a ring of light around the water's edge,
just dots in the distance.

I see my sons
and their friends.

Strangers
sit down on the sand
and stare silently into the flames,
imagining shapes,
just as men and women did
thousands of years ago.

The Tears of St Lawrence

to Analía Pascaner

A friend of mine
who lives in Argentina
says that watching the stars
makes her dizzy

that when she looks up
a star can appear

that when she sees one
above the mountains
it appears to disappear

and that the Milky Way
seems to move.

The sky has gone orange
over Swansea
but you can still see the stars
in Port Eynon.

I have counted
sixty burning tears of Saint Lawrence
falling from the sky
over the village.

The Photograph

I sat down
on the beach
in Port Eynon.

I put the photograph down
on the sand.

It was of a friend
and his father
by a lake.

I thought of Dylan
and his father
and of me and mine.

I fell asleep.

When I woke up
the tide had come in
and the photo
was disappearing
beneath the water.

The White Lady

to Ketty Lis

The night was as black as a bible.

We were driving down a lane in Wales

when I thought that I almost saw her in my headlights

the white lady

sitting on a gate.

I didn't know who she was

or what she meant.

She seemed to be mourning

the theft of the stone circle

from the field behind her.

Then I thought I saw Dylan

shuffling towards a village

in search of cigarettes from a machine that was

broken.

Then a barn owl with white wings

as broad as my car

attracted by my lights

swooped down, nearly smashing the windscreen.

I stopped

there was nothing.

I don't know what this means

but I can intuit it.

A friend of mine, who lives in Rosario,

says the white lady is poetry.

I remember having seen her

once

in a poem by Rimbaud

about a waterfall.

I must look for the book by Robert Graves

about this.

On Llanmadoc Hill

to Sir Cedric Lockwood Morris (1889-1982)

Sitting here
with my laptop
on Llanmadoc Hill,
looking at a painting,
'Llanmadoc Hill',
by Cedric Morris,
I start to wonder.

I wonder
if Dylan ever sat here.

I wonder if,
on one of his 'medicinal walks',
he looked down from here
upon Llanmadoc village.

I wonder
if he ever wondered
about an older name for the village:
Llanmadog, with a 'g'.

14

I wonder

if he looked down at the pond

by the farmhouse

and wondered what Llanmadog

would look like

when reflected in it, backwards.

"Godamnall."

I wonder if he was ever tempted

to use it in a play.

I wonder if he felt

that that, perhaps,

would have been too risky

and went for 'Llareggub',

buggerall backwards,

instead.

Heron's Way

I have stood
on a many a rainy day
at the window of Heron's Way,
the garage at the crossroads in Llanriddian,
staring out across the bleak expanse
of Burry Estuary and Camarthen Bay
but it wasn't until yesterday,
that I saw, sunlit,
Laugharne's
little inlet.

It wasn't until then
that I realised
that I had often looked
at the very place where Dylan lies,
with the Preseli Mountains
as his backdrop.

"Where?" I asked Lawrence,
squinting through squally showers,
as if through a telescopic gunsight
at the distant coast.
16

"There, in a straight line,
between the trees on Berges Island
and the cast-iron Victorian lighthouse
off Whiteford Point."

"I can't see any buildings," I said.

"You can on a clear day," he replied.

"Keep going along that line
and you'll end up in Fishguard
and Ireland.

It's funny
how you can go through life
without ever really seeing things
as they really are.

Dylan's Bay

I rang
the monumental mason
on my mobile
to discuss the wording
on my mother-in-law's tomb.

He said he was working
in the most beautiful spot
in the world
overlooking Swansea Bay.

He was in
Oystermouth Cemetery
not that far
from Dylan's house.

Some say it is as beautiful
as the Bay of Naples.

Dylan's Causeway

Tide rushing in,
pools filling up,
rocks sticking out,
not going to make it,
slithering and sliding,
panic rising,
Caitlin calling,
Wyn Lewis grinning,
old fear rising,
shoes filling up,
water up to knees,
legs turning to lead,
panting and grasping
at Vernon's helping hand;

feeling, for a moment,
as Illtyd did,
on stopping the incoming tide
from flooding his fertile fields
in Llanriddian.

Then the sodden posing,
Gwen Watkins saying cheese,
the clicking of the camera,
the sulking sinking
into a sullen gathering
of green-eyed gloom.

Dylan and the Monster

He was tired,
he needed to escape
from the whirlpool of the world.

He needed somewhere to lay his head,
just for a while perhaps,
somewhere,
anywhere where he could rest
and find new inspiration.

He saw the isolated Old Rectory
in Rhossili Bay.

But he was told, I imagine,
that, in mid-winter,
the ghost of a monstrous figure
with a revolting head,
like a distorted dollar sign,
like the ones on Viking ships' prows,
would rise up from the western waves

and cross the Dollar Ship beach.

He was told
that inside the Rectory itself
he would find himself wading
in pools of cold evil.

He was told that he would hear
a frightening voice that would call out:
"Dylan, why don't you turn round
and look at me?"
and that if he did,
he would find nothing there.

Obeying another call,
he turned away and went back to New York
where he died.

The Old Rectory

To Robert House

I went back to Rhossili
and sat on the cliff.

I stared at the place
where Dylan was tempted to live
in the very year that he died.

I recalled the story
that I had once been told
of the vicar who claimed
that he had heard footsteps
on its stairs.

I remembered that he and his wife
had gone to see who was there
and had witnessed two ghostly figures
with thick parchment-like skin
slide slowly towards them
before vanishing into thin air.

They were the ghosts,
I was told by a poet in Rhossili,
of a man and a woman
wearing Edwardian clothes.

The Gwrach-y-Rhibyn

I have never been
to the very end of The Worm.

I have never sat
amongst the herring gulls,
the guillemots, the razorbills
and the kittiwakes.

I have never been cut off for the night
by the incoming tide
on the Outer Head
as Dylan once was.

I find it hard to imagine
the fear he felt
of rats, bats and puffins.

What really went on
in his mind
when he was stranded that night
on the Inner Head of The Worm?

Did he imagine

that he might be scratched

by a 'Hag of the Rags',

a Gwrach-y-rhibyn,

with leathery wings

and terrible claws,

like the one he had heard about

down the coast,

the one who guards Pennard Castle,

the one with one blue eye

and the other grey?

Did he fear

that the ragged hag

would drive him mad?

We shall never know.

All that we know

is that he feared being attacked

by 'things of which

he was ashamed to be frightened'.

A Son's Dream

to my son William

We were walking
through the waves
on the beach in Port Eynon
without a care
in the world.

We didn't see it coming,
the tsunami.

We were pointing at tall stones
that had been carved into statues
standing in the water
some distance
from the shore.

One of them
looked like Dylan.

Then it hit us.

I was hurled
onto the rocks.

My brother
and his friend
were sucked out.

Everybody disappeared
but me,
under the waves.

I ran into the water
to try to rescue my brother
and his girl friend
but they were nowhere
to be seen.

One by one
people started bobbing up
gasping for air.

I had almost given up hope

when they reappeared

and threw themselves

on to the ground

on a mound

behind the Salt House.

The Slade

I had a dream this morning.

It was one of those dreams you have
when you are not quite sure
if you are asleep
or awake.

I felt that I was awake,
that I was really there.

Yet something told me
that it could not be so,
that I was here,
in Hertfordshire.

I am walking down a path.

It is one of those places
carved out by glaciers,
too big to be called a gulley,
too small to pass as a valley.

30

In that part of Gower
they are called slades.

It was quite clear to me
that it was Long Hole Bay.

I was going down to the sea.

The going wasn't easy.

I found myself caught up
in a bed of nettles.

My feet kept getting trapped
under low-lying brambles
that looked crushed and dead.

I had a feeling
that there had a been a fire
but that the sea air and the wind
had dispersed the ashes.

The words 'bremmels' and 'vurzey sticks',
and other bits of the local dialect

are buzzing in my head now.
Beneath the tangle
of twisted, blackened branches
my feet can feel the scree,
the stones and rocks
that are creeping down the hillsides.

For me,
it is one of the most peaceful places
on earth.

The slade gets wider
as I descend.

The sea and its yachts are framed
by the V-shape of the cliffs.

All I can sea is the sea.

All I can hear are the waves
and the cries of mew gulls.

The water sparkles
in the midday sun.

It is impossible not to think
of Sète and Paul Valéry's
Cemetery by The Sea.

I can see a familiar shape there,
sitting on a want-'eap,
his chin cupped
in his hands.

I went to my desk
and the dream receded
but it kept clambering
to be seen.

I came to a difficult decision
that leaves me full of guilt.

I am not going to translate that novel,

Vallejo en los infiernos,

Vallejo in Hell.

The Shepherd

I used to see him
tending his sheep
in a field above Port Eynon.

We would talk about Dylan.

He told me with pride
that he had preached in Welsh
at the funeral of a friend
in the Church
of Saint Catwgg.

Then he said
that someone had asked him afterwards
why the devil he had used
that 'foreign' language.

A few months later
they found him in his house
at the top of the cliff
hanging by the neck.
34

A Premonition

Phantoms and Tornadoes
fill the skies
above Port Eynon.

Two crows
attack a swallow.

There is something
in the air.

Moonrise

The moon rose red
last night
over the Bristol Channel.

Then it turned orange
and plunged upwards
into a bank of black cloud.

Cefn Bryn

Yesterday a jet
roared across the sky
just a few feet
above the heather
on Cefn Bryn.

I read in a paper
that in Teheran
they had changed the name
of Winston Churchill Street
to that of Bobby Sands.

The Heron

There is a heron
in a pool
at the side of the road
that crosses
the empty plain
in Gower.

It doesn't see Dylan
passing by,
climbing Cefn Bryn.

The Poundffald

They say that Dylan's ghost

can be seen now and then

in The White Horse Tavern

in New York

spinning his favourite table

the way he loved to do

and that his head can be seen

floating in front of a mirror

or just watching you

from the end of your bed

in a room

in the Chelsea Hotel.

I don't know exactly

where Dylan liked to sit

in the Poundffald Inn.

I like to think
that it was there,
in the circular corner,
where the village pound
used to be.

That's where I see him.

A friend of mine in Wernffrwd
lives by a stream
where otters stray down from a hill
to steal her fish.

She says that her uncle
used to see him there,
in the Poundffald,
looking lost
and 'worse for wear'.

Chatterpies

In Overton Village,
above Port Eynon,
there's an isolated house
called 'Chatterpie's Nest'.

I used to see myself
as a magpie fluttering down,
snapping up anything shiny,
rings and things ,
through open windows.

Then I saw
that someone
in Delvid by Broughton Bay
was shooting magpies
and hanging them on a fence
for stealing the eyes
of new-born lambs.

The Britannia

"Was Dylan ever here?"
I asked some people
in The Britannia Inn
in Llanmadoc.

"Some say he was,
some say he wasn't",
came the reply.

The King's Head

I looked in through the window
of 'The King's Head'
in Llangennith
and I thought that I saw Dylan
sitting on the stairs,
by himself,
with his head
in his hands.

The White Lady of Oystermouth Castle

Ghosts whooed like owls in the long nights

when I dared not look over my shoulder.

'A Child's Christmas in Wales'

It's strange to think

that there was so much going on

not much more than a stone-throw

from Dylan's window.

I don't know

if he knew about it.

I don't know if he knew

about the murder holes and the missiles,

the burning tar and the quicklime,

the boiling oil and the burning sand,

the scalding water

that was poured down on

enemy soldiers.

I don't know if he knew
about the whipping post
that can still be seen
by the dungeon.

Neither do I know if he knew
about the ghost of the White Lady
that belongs to a woman
who was whipped to death
in Oystermouth Castle.
There is no record that I know of
of his ever having seen
her naked, lacerated back,
nor even the white sheet on the ground
that rises
and takes the form of a woman in a white robe
before finally vanishing
into the mist.

I don't know if he ever heard dogs barking wildly
when they are walked past a certain tree.

Some say she is called
The Grey Lady of Oystermouth,
not The White.

Some say she was grey
and that she can be seen
walking through the wall
with her head in her hands..

Some say, in fact,
that hundreds have seen her
turn her back on them
and show them her wounds.

Words on Water

I dreamt last night
of somebody.

I think it was Dylan.

He had a fishing net in his hand
like the ones children sometimes use
to catch butterflies.

The words
"Rage, rage, against the dying of the light".
and "Do not go gentle into that good night",
were floating down
the slow-flowing stream.

I think it was Dylan
but it may have been Francis Bacon,
or me as a child,
or even me now,
- I can't remember -

squatting there by the water,

catching the letters

and putting them in a pile

next to me

on the river bank

higgledy-piggledy.

(River Lliw, Pont-Y-Cob)

Under Milk Wood

I was talking to a solicitor
who lives near Llareggub,
a man who looks after
the wills and deeds
of the rural aristocracy.
He shoots ducks.

I asked him what he thought
of Dylan Thomas

He answered
that he had just seen
Under Milk Wood
in the Grand Theatre in Swansea
and, frankly.
he had not liked it.

I don't know why,
something in his manner, perhaps,
but I didn't ask him why.

5 Cymdonkin Drive

I was in Dylan's house
in Cymdonkin Drive.

The first thing I was asked to do
was to close my eyes,
go back in time
and imagine an Edwardian house,
brand new.

I saw Dylan's parents
sitting there by the range
in the kitchen.

I saw them lying
in their bed.

I saw his sister
lying in hers
and Dylan
lying on his.

50

I saw the packet of Woodbines.

I saw uncles nodding off
by the fire in the front room.

The whole family appeared
then faded away.

It was as if I had entered
a sepia-coloured world.

It didn't feel right.
I felt like a voyeur.
I felt that I was intruding.
I felt that I had no right
to be there.

Swansea Calling

to Andrés Bohoslavsky

It's strange
how we sometimes hear voices
repeating themselves
in our heads.

A friend of mine
sent me an e-mail
saying that he was approaching
'Cipo', pronounced 'Cheep-Oh'
short for Cipolletti,
in Patagonia.

I thought of the newspaper seller
who stood outside The Quadrant,
the Shopping Centre,
in Swansea,
whose voice could be heard
a block or more away.

He would shout out "EE-PO"
("Evening Post").
Perhaps he still does.

I remembered
how I had once said to my friend
in Cipoletti
that the newsvendor's words
seemed to fly over the ocean
to Argentina.

My friend told me
that he had just heard him calling
on the corner, by the flea-pit
where he was staying.

But the words, he said,
were different:
"Ipo and Cipo,
karma and dharma for all."

The Worm's Head Hotel

I had a message today
from Catamarca
in Argentina.

In it my friend said
that she loved her mountains,
that they change colour
according to the time of day
but that today
she could not see them
behind the clouds.

She had to imagine them.

She also seemed sad
that she didn't know
about an ancestor
called Heller.

I told her

that I knew a man
called Heller
who ran a hotel on top of the cliff
at Worm's Head
in Gower.

I told her how once
he opened the door of the bar
and shook his fist
at a hang glider pilot
who was hovering
too near his windows.

"You're banned",
he shouted.

Today he lies in the cemetery
of St Mary's Church
overlooking Rhossili Bay
the most beautiful bay
in the world,
some locals say.

I told her he knew Dylan.

Walking The Worm

I am on Worm's Head,
standing under a wooden sign
in the shape of a hand with a pointing finger
that says 'Patagonia 8000 miles'.

I hear an Argentine voice.
He is on his mobile.
He is wearing binoculars
slung around his neck.

"Excuse me, "I ask him,
"Can you tell me the collective nouns
for birds in Spanish?"

He studies me for moment,
his tongue whetting his lips.
He's thirsty, I think.

"Well", he begins,
"We've got flocks of birds
and flights of birds.
I don't know, we don't have many."
56

"Don't you say a congregation of plovers,
or 'little brothers ',
over there?"
I ask him,
nodding towards the horizon.

"No, nothing like that.
I have never heard that",
he replies.

"We say a fall of leaves,
a denture of teeth,
a herd of animals."

"You don't say
a parliament of rooks?"

"No, no", he titters,
"a parliament of fools, perhaps".

I didn't know whether to smile.
Would it be undiplomatic?

We say 'una alameda',

for a grove of poplars,

an anthill of ants,

a rose-garden of roses."

"No, no, birds", I insist.

"Don't you say a charm of goldfinches

for several *jilgueros*?"

"No, no," he replies , "a flock'.

We say a grove of trees,

an archipelago of islands,

an army of soldiers,

a squadron of aircraft.

Al that stuff with birds

is a British curiosity.

The conversation is taking

a turn for the worse, I feel.

I change the subject.

"Why don't we pop in for a jar,

over there,

in The Worm's Head Hotel?"

I suggest.

"I don't mind if I do",

he replies.

Rhossili Bay

I have been told that on certain nights
you can see the ghost of a Rhossili vicar
by the name of Lucas
riding a black horse on the sands.

I have been told that on stormy nights
a black coach will appear
with four grey horses.

I have been told that you can see
the ghost of one Squire Mansell
sitting on the coach,
whipping the horses,
that he returns on dark nights
to search for more coins
from the wreck of a ship.

I have been told
that the vessel that went down
was carrying Catherine of Braganza's dowry.
I don't know if Dylan was told these tales
but I imagine he was.

60

The Da Vinci Code

On the cliffs

in the distance

above the village of Horton

huge cows

magnified

by a trick of the light

are eating the grass.

On the beach

below the trees

where Dylan once sat

beautiful women in bikinis

are reading a book

that some say

is full of lies.

Port Eynon From Space

to Vicente Huidobro

The sun is setting.
The sky is cloudless.
The earth looks beautiful.
Half of it is in darkness.
Its cities are bright dots.
The lights are on
in Barcelona and Paris.
It is still daylight
in London and Madrid.
The sun is still shining
in Ceuta and Gibraltar.
It's night time
in the Mediterranean.
In the middle of the Atlantic
you can see the Azores.
Below them, to the right,
is Madeira
Further down are the Canaries.
Close to Africa,

you can see Cape Verde Islands.

The Sahara is huge

and can be seen

even at night.

To the left, on top,

is Greenland,

totally frozen.

There's a flash of light in Port Eynon,

as I open the bedroom window

to let a butterfly out.

Did you see it, Vicente?

Dylan Down Here

I was tempted
to dedicate my poem
'Port Eynon From Space'
to Dylan.

But I thought, somehow,
that it wouldn't be right.

I wanted to ask him
if he could see
how beautiful Gower looks
when seen from space.

But then I remembered
that Dylan used to tumble about
in the here and now,
in the undergrowth
below the cliff.

I am not sure
that he was ever up there
in space
with Vicente Huidobro.

He spent more time
down here, I think,
walking by the stream
that fed his uncle's mill
in Kingsbridge.

On The Point

I met him on top
of Port Eynon Point.

He had all the trappings
of a bird watcher.

I asked him if he knew
the collective nouns for birds.

"A charm of goldfinches,
a covert of coots,
a train of jackdaws
a clattering of choughs,"
he began.

"Ah, choughs," I interrupted.
"We haven't see those for years."
I was testing him.

He told me that he had seen them
that very same day,

66

on the cliffs between Overton
and Worm's Head.

He said they had returned
from Cornwall.

"A tiding of magpies,
a herd of wrens,
a parliament of rooks
and a nide of pheasants,"
he went on.

"A nide of pheasants?" I asked,
"where have you seen them
in the Gower Peninsula"

"Back there, in Middleton,"
he replied.
"There's a chap there
who breads them for shoots."

"A congregation of plovers,
a building of rooks,
an unkindness of ravens
and a siege of bitterns."

He paused for breath.

"Where have you seen bitterns?"
I asked him.
"Surely they went long ago.

"No, they are back," he said,
"on Oxwich Marsh."

"Isn't it a sedge of bitterns?"
I asked,
searching for a chink
in his armour.

The question threw him a little.

"Ah, a siege of herons,
a sedge of herons, a siege of bitterns,
a sedge of bittern," he chanted,
as if trying to remember.

He was still talking to himself
as he went down the steep path
that leads to Port Eynon:

68

"A kettle of buzzards,

a dole of doves,

a rasp of guinea fowl,

a watch of nightingales,

a flight of swallows,

a drift of quail."

Imagine

What does it feel like
in Africa?
my sons and their friends
once asked me
as we made castles
and animals on the sand
on the beach in Port Eynon.

Imagine, I said,
that you came face to face
with a red-necked wallaby.

It wouldn't be too bad.

Imagine that you found yourselves
standing next to a ring-tailed lemur,
a Chinese muntjac
or a bar-headed goose.
You can, at Whipsnade Zoo,
near Luton.

70

It feels fine.
But imagine that you are on a road
in the north of Uganda
and an elephant takes umbrage
at having to share
the same space with you.

Or a row of buffaloes
suddenly emerges
from a forest in Rwanda
just as you have set off
to do some exploring.

Or a black mamba snake
lies curls up in your porch
just before the ten o'clock curfew
and there are soldiers in the road
clicking their guns outside your flat
by Lugard's Fort in Kampala.

It's not quite the same
when there are no bars, no glass, no wire
between you and them.
The feeling is different.
It doesn't feel that good.

The Peacock's Tail

You can get close to nature
on the Gower peninsula.

The rain, in summer, is warm

You can walk round a hedge
on a cliff above Port Eynon
and come face to face
with a black and white cow.

It can make you jump.

You can smell its breath.
You can see your reflection
in its eye.

As a boy Dylan liked the experience
of lying on his stomach
in the warm hay
in a field near Pilton
and reading his early poems

from his first notebook

to a pretty girl

called Evelyn,

while others made hay.

Foxhole Bay

I wanted to write a poem today
about Caitlin doing cartwheels
on the beach in Foxhole Bay.

I wanted to talk about her beauty
her golden hair, her light blue eyes,
her firm, rosy cheeks.

I wanted to explore the similarity
between her and Blodeuwedd,
the flower lady of the Mabinogion.

I wanted to find out why
Blodeuwedd was turned into an owl
by a wizard called Gwydion.

I was drawn instead
to an image in my mind
of Caitlin and her daughter
spearing flatfish through their toes
in Laugharne's muddy water,
while Dylan looked on.

The White Lady of Caswell Bay

They say
that a witch
fashions the sand into castles
in Caswell Bay.

They say
that they can withstand
the movement
of the tides.

They say
that if you look closely
you can see
her invisible hands.

I am not so sure
that they are hers.

I like to think
that they belong
to someone else.

The Way We Are Now

You go down to Wales
to the house of your wife's parents
in the village by the sea
where people seem as large
as the characters in *Under Milk Wood*
where everyone knows everyone
and where they notice
if even a blade of grass
has been moved.

The sun and sea-bleached statue of Billy Gibbs,
the lifeboat man who died saving others,
is always there,
just by the Church of St Cattwg,
looking out over the bay
and at people who come and go.

You go down now and then,
in the school holidays,
with the children,
whenever you can.

You make friends with a German family
you never see again.

You strike up a friendship
with a Danish violinist
who never returns.

There was that French family who said
that it is better
than the south of France.
They didn't come back.

And there was that nice family
from South-East London
who now go now to a 'better' village
nearer to Rhossili.

But you feel at home.

Sometimes there is a gap,
something comes up
that stops you getting down.

The car's playing up.
A friend you haven't seen
for twenty years
is coming from Bilbao.

Someone you have never met
but with whom you exchange e-mails
is coming from Buenos Aires.

Someone falls ill.
You can't get away.

You stay at home.

And then you go back
and ask "How is old Myfanwy
from Mumbles?"

"Oh, didn't you know,
she died last winter,
aged ninety-two."

"And how is The Reverend Jenkins?"
"Oh, he died too."

"And what about The Captain
who was always in The Ship?"
"He passed away last summer."

"And Mrs Beynon?"
"She's gone too."

"And Mr Pugh in the big house?"
"He died in Malta."

"And Mr Ogmore
who cut the grass in the graveyard?"
"Gone."

They all had big funerals
and you just didn't know.

We were all once like that,
like those people in that village
under the cliff.

The Way I Am Now

You make friends with a couple
who were proud to have slept
in the bed in the Bed and Breakfast
where John Lennon and Yoko Ono
had once made love.

They never returned.

You go back and ask,
How is dear old Angharad
who had much more than a soft spot
for Dylan Thomas?

She died last year,
one hundred and two.

And Mr Morgan the plumber
who sat on the bench at the sea-front
with his bible on his lap
and loved to prophesy
the end of the world?

No more.

And Mr Williams with his two sticks

who ruined his legs

rescuing sheep from snowdrifts

up on the cliff

in that bad winter of '79

and who rang the church bell?

Gone.

But the bell still rings.

And the Reverend Hopkins

who was so massive

that he needed to wear

two suits stitched together?

He died last May.

And that angry Dai Breathalyser,

the policeman,

who spoke Welsh

and was sent to Coventry

by the villagers
for making dark noises
about Welsh Nationalism?

And Betty Harry
who delivered the papers?

No. Her tiny house
is now a private garage.

Alas, no more.

And those tourists
from the former East Germany
with their battered car
who wouldn't talk
about politics?

And that large Hasidic family
from London
who would bathe fully dressed
at full tide?

You begin to forget their names.
They begin to sink into anonymity,

as you, no doubt, do, for them.

It's nobody's fault.
It's the way things are now.

It's strange
but, in a way,
I quite like the anonymity of it all.

You can get used to it.
It's the way we are being made.

Like my favourite poets,
I, too, perhaps, on balance,
prefer to be anonymous.

The Three Wise Monkeys

I was astonished to see them there
in the shop window:

"See no evil, hear no evil, speak no evil."

They were shaped like dragons.

Then I saw three cherubs and three toads.

There was a picture
of three monkeys in the Sacred Stable,
the Nikko Toshogo Shrine,
in Japan.

I went inside and found a post card
of the Chinese Buddhist monk
who had introduced the three wise monkeys
into Japan
twelve hundred years ago.

For him

they were connected with

a blue-faced deity called Vadjra

who had many hands

and whose main tenet was:

"Hear no evil, see no evil, speak no evil

and no evil will befall you."

How can I tell my friends in Patagonia,

three brothers at war,

that they need to sit and talk

and let it all out?

How can I tell them

that they need to say what they feel

about their father's death

in the nineteen seventies?

How can I tell them

that it is this inability to talk

that is causing their problem?

I kept looking

for the three monkeys in Swansea

but I couldn't find them,
just toads, cherubs and dragons.
Then, one day, I went
into the sea-front shop in Port Eynon,
and saw them there,
high up, jet-black,
carved out of coal.

They were joined together.
Each seemed to be facing
a different way.

I bought three.

I haven't sent them yet
to Patagonia.

It is all just a little bit too difficult.

I wrote this poem instead
but I still haven't sent it.

Alien Stones

The tide rose again today
in Port Eynon Bay
bringing a dead angler fish,
and a tin can from Brazil.

Yesterday
the tide went out so far
that the beach looked like
a desert.

And there,
amongst the rocks,
I found small pieces of copper
from a ship that was wrecked
off Port Eynon Point
trying to get to get back to Swansea
from Sardinia
or Peru.

In the distance I could see,

lying on the sand, oval, blue-black,

the 'alien stones' from Devon

that were carried once as ballast

in the sailing ships

that came to collect

oysters, sheep

and lime.

Arthur's Stone

I have heard it said
that, at full moon,
young women would crawl three times
around or under Arthur's Stone
where Dylan once sat.

They say they would place
an offering upon the stone:
a cake made with barley and honey
and wetted with milk.

It is said that they were testing
their lovers' fidelity
and that if he appeared
before they had finished
he would stay faithful for life.

I read somewhere else
that they just wanted
to get pregnant.

The Cask of Ale that Never Runs Dry

There is no way
that I can believe the rumour
that Dylan went looking for
a magic cask of ale
in Lagadranta.

I can believe
that he was told the story
of the fairy who asked a farmer's wife
for the loan of a sieve
so that she could go
looking for gold.

He would have heard the story
in The Dolphin,
in The Britannia,
or in The King's Head.

It is possible
that someone told him

90

that the farmer's wife
had told the little old woman
that she had no sieve
and that the little old lady said
that, yes, she did have one,
for straining the hops.

It is possible that he heard
that the farmer's wife suddenly realised
that she was in the presence of
one of the Verry Volk
and had handed over the sieve.

If he had
his ears would have pricked up
on hearing that,
on returning the sieve,
the fairy had promised
that the farm's largest cask of ale
would never run dry
provided the farmer's wife swore
never to tell a soul.

He would have heard
that all went swimmingly

until one day

the secret was leaked

and the pot dried up.

It is possible

that Dylan knew this story.

It's in all the old guide books.

I am not so sure

that I believe the rumour

that he was seen in Lagadranta

looking for the fairy.

Why in this world,

I ask you, dear reader,

would Dylan have wanted

a cask of ale that never ran dry?

Dylan Playing

It's strange
to think
that Dylan
used to walk
up and down the river bank
and play in the hay
behind the Kingsbridge Inn,
the Tafarn-y-Trap pub
and Ken Pollard's Dance School
in Gorseinon,
there where
they are building
a village
of expensive houses.

The Vicar in the Park

Gloveless old ladies sit,
loveless,
peering at an old paper
that lies at their feet.

The first heaps of leaves,
withered brown, breast-like,
punctuate the park's path.

Inside the Gorsedd Stone Ring
a solitary vicar kicks
at this cornflake leaf and that,
searching for inspiration.

He is preparing a sermon.
He has been asked
to preach about Dylan.

Ideas swirl around in his head.

He remembers the story,
still circulating in Gorseinon,
about Dylan and his wife
lying in a ditch near Pembrey
unable to get out.

He likes a drink himself.

'Let him who is without sin.'

"No, that won't do!"
 he mutters.

He pictures Dylan
marooned on Worm's Head.
He feels his fear.
He shudders at the thought
of rats, bats and adders
brushing against him
in the moonless night.

How can he tie that
to the story of a child
thrown into the Lliw river
then cast up in an osier basket

onto the Crabbart rocks

of The Worm?

Did that dreadful deed

take place, in actual fact,

in Gorseinon?

How can he weave in a mention

of Arthur's Court

in Loughor?

How can he find the words

to describe the horror felt

by the parents of Saint Cenydd

when they saw that the calf

on their newborn baby's leg

was attached to the thigh?

How can he describe their conviction

that it was a punishment

by an angry God

for their terrible sin?

Cennyth's mother was his sister!

How can he even describe
the enormity of the crime
of allowing a tiny infant to die
on the open sea?

How can he bring in the miracle
of the'titty bell'?

How can he begin to tell his flock
that a large breast-shaped bell
carried by sea-gulls
descended from heaven
and dripped milk
through its hollow handle
into the mouth
of the abandoned child?

How can tell his parishioners
that those very same gulls
lifted the boy up from the waves
and took him to safety on Worm's Head,
tearing the very feathers from their chests
to make a bed for him to lie on?

How can he allude to the fact

that a doe, emerging from a wood,
continued to fill
the bosom-like bell,
the Cloch Dethog,
with its milk?

How can he disentangle
such a kaleidoscope of symbols?

How can he say
that the saint's clothes
grew at the same rate
as he did?

How can he refer to the fact
that the child was instructed
by angels?

Who would believe him?

There would be late holiday-makers
in the pews.

He raises his eyes to the skies.
He searches the clouds for an answer.

98

Nothing –
just the inverted commas
of wind-tossed mewgulls' wings
with a blank space in-between.

He remembers that Saint Cenydd
lived cut off on Burry Holmes.

He explores the link
between a strong spirit
and the wilderness.

He remembers Jesus's forty days
in the wild.

Dylan on Ynysweryn, Snake Island,
Cenydd on Ynys Ianwol.

"Ianwol?
What does Ianwol mean?"
He is talking to himself.

The ideas will not come.

The wind begins to blow
as he hurries towards the safety
of the dark porch of his church.

Then something in the park
reminds him of the nests
hanging rook-black, like wicker baskets,
in the trees near the King Arthur.

He remembers Dylan's fondness
for his aunts.

He remembers the old lullaby:

'Rock-a-bye baby, on the treetop,
When the wind blows, the cradle will rock,
When the bough breaks, the cradle will fall,
And down will come baby, cradle and all.'

The words begin to sing
in his mind.
 He enters his church.
The organ is playing.

Old ladies nod a greeting.

"Today the family, *a* family
and *the* family", he proclaims,
smiling at his congregation,
as he walks on to the stage
in front of the altar.

Milk Under Wood

Sitting here
on this hill
above Llanrhiddian
I explore, in my mind,
the tunnels
that run through the limestone
beneath my feet.

I see the invisible
Llanrhiddian stream.

I see a collapsing
underground cave.

I look down
towards the Butter Well
where, I am told,
milk bubbled up
a thousand years ago.

They say
that it flowed continuously
for up to three hours.

They say
that fatty curds could be seen
lying on the gravel.

Sitting here
in this wood
of Gower Sub Boscus
I explore an idea,
that the milk of St Illtyd's well
may have found its way
into the churning urn
of Dylan's subconscious.

The Milk of Milk Wood

We sat there for hours
talking about Dylan.

He asked me how Dylan
had chosen the title
for *Under Milk Wood*.

I described how John Malcolm Brinnin
had asked him in Laugharne
to drop the "too thick and forbidding" title
of *Llareggub*
and how Dylan had volunteered
on the spot
"Under Milk Wood"
and how this was accepted with a brief
"Fine"
from the American.

I explained my Freudian theory
about the milk in *Under Milk Wood*.

We discussed Saint John's Hill
104

and its cows in Laugharne.
I recited my poem from *To Dylan*
about the magnified cows
on the cliffs in Horton.
I said that cows like that
could be seen all round Gower.

I mentioned the titty bell
that descended from the sky
dripping milk
into Saint Kenneth's mouth.

I brought in the milk
that was later supplied to the saint
by a doe that emerged
from a wood in West Gower.

We discussed the milk
that flowed from the Butter Well
in Llanrhidian many years ago.

I offered a scientific explanation.

I described the wood
on the hill above the village.

"That's it!" he exclaimed.
"But what does it mean?"

"What do you mean what does it mean?"
I asked.

"The milk, what does it mean?"

"It comes from the ground,
from a hidden realm," I said.
"It comes from Dylan's subconscious.
The images that emerge from that well
poured out onto his page.
They were the milk that sustained him,
the milk of the land that nourished him,
the land of South Wales,
the earth of Gower Sub Boscus
that formed him and shaped
his early imagination.

In the past inspiration
came from above.

For Dylan and the Surrealists
it came from below.

106

The Water Horse

I don't know why
and I don't know what it can mean
but my wife used to have a dream
that she was riding a wild horse
across Oxwich marsh.

It was, she tells me,
a recurring nightmare.

Today I heard
that a white water horse,
was once was seen
in the churchyard of St Illtyd's
before it disappeared
down the now dried-up well.

Some say the ceffyl dŵr
would invite unwary travelers
to jump onto his back
and ride him through the sky.

They say that he could then
evaporate, leaving the rider
to fall to his or her death.

"Beware the handsome stranger",
my wife's mother used to tell her.

Today, as I watch the spindrift streaming
from white horses in the bay,
I wonder if Dylan ever wondered
where his winged Pegasus
would eventually let him fall.

By the same author:

La poesía de Juan Larrea

Poemas a la Patagonia

Luton Poems

Nueve monedas para el barquero

El cuarto oscuro y otros poemas

La libélula y otros poemas / The Dragonfly and Other Poems

La casa de empeño y otros poemas / The Pawn Shop and Other Poems

A Night in Buganda: Tales from Post-Colonial Africa

To Dylan

Translation: The River and Other Poems (Andrés Bohoslavsky)

Comment on To Dylan:

"A lovely, touching tribute." (John Goodby)

"I like your light touch and gentle humour." (Robert Havard)

"As only happens with true poetry, I know I will never stop reading it." (Ramón Minieri)

"Stunning ... you have a wonderful, magical quality in your words ... " (Tom Scott, Richard Burton Museum)

To Dylan is published by Cambria Books.
ISBN: 978-0-9928690-3-8

See the author's website : www.verpress.com for more information